"Grow in the grace and
knowledge of our Lord
and Savior Jesus Christ."

2 Peter 3:18

Elizabeth Smith

God Speaks

through

Ordinary Things

ELIZABETH SMITH

Inspiring Voices®

Scripture taken from the Holy Bible, NEW INTERNATIONAL VERSION®. Copyright © 1973, 1978, 1984 by Biblica, Inc. All rights reserved worldwide. Used by permission. NEW INTERNATIONAL VERSION® and NIV® are registered trademarks of Biblica, Inc. Use of either trademark for the offering of goods or services requires the prior written consent of Biblica US, Inc.

Inspiring Voices books may be ordered through booksellers or by contacting:

Inspiring Voices
1663 Liberty Drive
Bloomington, IN 47403
www.inspiringvoices.com
1 (866) 697-5313

Because of the dynamic nature of the Internet, any web addresses or links contained in this book may have changed since publication and may no longer be valid. The views expressed in this work are solely those of the author and do not necessarily reflect the views of the publisher, and the publisher hereby disclaims any responsibility for them.

Any people depicted in stock imagery provided by Thinkstock are models, and such images are being used for illustrative purposes only. Certain stock imagery © Thinkstock.

ISBN: 978-1-4624-1092-7 (sc)
ISBN: 978-1-4624-1091-0 (e)

Library of Congress Control Number: 2014922220

Printed in the United States of America.

Inspiring Voices rev. date: 01/22/2015

To Hermann and Elisabeth Bottcher. They were
devoted servants of Christ. An opportunity to
speak for Christ was never overlooked. Their faith
never wavered through all their adversities.

Thank you, Jerry Crossley, for encouraging me to write this book. I thank my sister, Margaret McDowell, and my three daughters, Kathy Mehr, Lois Hendrickson, and Margaret Christensen, for their input and encouragement. Thank you, R. Gilbert Leeds, for helping make sure that what is written is biblically correct.

Contents

Introduction

When we take the time to stop and listen, we can hear God giving us a message in the ordinary things and happenings of life.

"Listen, my son, and be wise, and set your heart on the right path" (Proverbs 23:19).

All verses are taken from the New International Version of the Bible, except where noted.

Geritol's Advertisement

Do not add to what I command you and do
not subtract from it, but keep the commands
of the LORD your God that I give you.
—Deuteronomy 4:2

G eritol's ad says, "Complete for what's in it; special for what's not."

The same slogan could be applied to the Bible. The Bible is complete, affirming that we are all sinners and telling of God's provision so everyone can be saved. "For all have sinned and fall short of the glory of God" (Romans 3:23).

It states the only way of salvation. "Jesus answered, 'I am the way and the truth and the life. No one comes to the Father except through me'" (John 14:6).

It tells you the way you should conduct your life. "So whether you eat or drink or whatever you do, do it all for the glory of God" (1 Corinthians 10:31).

The Bible is also special for what it does not say. It does not say you need to or can earn your way to heaven. It is a free gift. Ephesians 2:8–9 tells us, "For it is by grace you have been saved, through faith—and this is not from yourselves, it is the gift of God—not by works, so that no one can boast."

The Bible tells you that you cannot add to or subtract from God's Word to match your lifestyle. "See that you do all I command you; do not add to it or take away from it" (Deuteronomy 12:32).

Even though God's Word was written many years ago, it hasn't changed and will never change. "Heaven and earth will pass away, but my words will never pass away" (Luke 21:33).

Jesus is inviting you today to come to Him and have eternal life. "'Come now, let us settle the matter,' says the LORD. 'Though your sins are like scarlet, they shall be as white as snow; though they are red as crimson, they shall be like wool'" (Isaiah 1:18).

Will you receive this free gift of God that He wants to give you?

Building a Modular Home

Now you are the body of Christ, and
each one of you is a part of it.
—1 Corinthians 12:27

I watched the progress of a modular home being erected. Pilings were pounded deep into the ground. The cement basement floor was poured and left to cure before the joints, beams, and flooring were put in place.

Each section of the house was brought on its own long tractor trailer. After the crane lifted the first section, the next truck pulled up. This was the procedure until all four parts were in place.

A huge, tall crane with two heavy straps was used to lift each section. These straps were securely wrapped around each end of the four segments. The straps held each portion securely and gently until they were over the right place and then nailed down.

A man standing on the ground held a long, strong cord attached to one corner of the section being lifted to help guide it as it passed the neighbor's home to avoid a collision.

The builder knew the exact size of the house. He also knew where to place the doors and windows so that the sections would line up perfectly with one another to complete the house.

God also knows what you can be and is working in all areas of your life to make you complete in Him.

The pilings pounded into the ground and the cement being cured, or hardened, before the house can be built are the same as studying, meditating on, and believing God's Word. Being grounded in what you read, you will not be swayed from the truth.

"Do your best to present yourself to God as one approved, a worker who does not need to be ashamed and who correctly handles the word of truth" (2 Timothy 2:15).

God, like the crane, holds you in His arms gently yet securely, lifting you up when the days are rough. "When I said, 'My foot is slipping,' your unfailing love, LORD, supported me" (Psalm 94:18).

As the man helps guide the sections, the Holy Spirit wants to guide you past many temptations and pitfalls.

Just as the trucks brought each part to be added to the house, you need to grow in faith and add knowledge, self-control, integrity, and kindness in your life. You need to persevere in obeying the Lord, in reading the Bible, and in prayer.

Are you being grounded and growing in your knowledge of God's Word?

The Heavens

By the word of the LORD the heavens were made,
their starry host by the breath of his mouth.
—Psalm 33:6

On the fourth day, the Lord spoke and created the sun to rule the day. He created the moon and stars to rule the night. The Lord separated the day from the night. God made the sun and moon for signs, days, seasons, and years. "He made the moon to mark the seasons" (Psalm 104:19).

God knows the number of stars He created and the name of each one. "He determines the number of stars and calls them each by name" (Psalm 147:4).

God keeps the heavens on schedule to this day. Before calendars were made, months could be counted by the position of the moon at night. Today, calendars can be printed in advance with the correct months, days, and dates. Even the phases of the moon can be printed on the correct date.

God also controls the weather. In the winter, He sends the snow, sleet, and ice storms. In the other seasons, He sends the clouds with rain, often accompanied by thunder and lightning.

God gives the cool, refreshing breezes on hot, sunny days in summer. The tornados, hurricanes, and floods are all under God's control.

After the flood destroyed everything except Noah, his family, and all the animals in the ark, God promised Noah never to flood the entire earth again. To commemorate His promise, God placed a rainbow in the sky. Often after it rains, a rainbow can be seen.

God, who still controls the whole universe—not only the earth, but all the planets and stars—loves you and pleads for you to come to Him.

"Here I am! I stand at the door and knock. If anyone hears my voice and opens the door, I will come in and eat with that person, and they with me" (Revelation 3:20).

Will you come to Him? What will be your answer?

Displaying God's Glory

The sky declares God's splendor
By the sun, clouds, moon, and stars.
The wind, sleet, snow, hail, and showers
All show God's magnificent powers.

The sun rises, lighting the sky,
Bursting into colors bright.
Then it sets in colors rare,
Turning day into night.

During the day, white clouds float
Across a wide blue spread.
At night, stars like shining diamonds
Gleam on a black velvet bed.

The clouds lower and darken.
Lightning streaks across the sky.
The wind howls from the north,
Whipping the waves up high.

Yes, the heavens declare God's glory
With all the elements at His command.

The Mountains

He who forms mountains, who creates the wind,
and who reveals his thoughts to mankind, who turns
dawn to darkness, and treads on the heights of the
earth—the LORD God Almighty is his name.
—Amos 4:13

Traveling through the midwestern states, I saw the vast difference between the Grand Canyon and the Zion, Bryce, and Red Canyons. From the northern rim of the Grand Canyon you need to look down to see the huge crater with strong purple walls. You need to look up to see the many different, odd, yet beautiful reddish rock formations in Zion, Bryce and Red Canyons.

These four canyons show God's wondrous and varied handiwork, which man cannot begin to duplicate. They also show His power to drastically change the landscape within miles.

Like many of the mountains surrounding towns and ranches, Jesus Christ surrounds His people, protecting them. "As the mountains surround Jerusalem, so the LORD surrounds his people both now and forevermore" (Psalm 125:2).

The towering, rugged mountains reaching down on each side of Virgin River Gorge's highway display strength and endurance and appear to be protecting everyone traveling through the gorge. Unlike these mountains, which only seem to be protecting everyone traveling through the gorge, God has the strength and everlasting power to protect you as you travel through life if you will let Him.

God has promised to take care of you even when you are old. He is always faithful. "Even to your old age and gray hairs I am he, I am he who will sustain you. I have made you and I will carry you; I will sustain you and I will rescue you" (Isaiah 46:4).

God's righteousness is stronger, higher, and wider than the mountains. Isaiah 40:28–29 tells us, "Do you not know? Have you not heard? The LORD is the everlasting God, the Creator of the ends of the earth. He will not grow tired or weary, and his understanding no one can fathom. He gives strength to the weary and increases the power of the weak."

Are you leaning on God's strength and faithfulness to help you every day?

The Ocean

"Should you not fear me?" declares the LORD.
"Should you not tremble in my presence? I made the
sand a boundary for the sea, an everlasting barrier it
cannot cross. The waves may roll, but they cannot
prevail; they may roar, but they cannot cross it."
—Jeremiah 5:22

S itting on the beach, I marveled how the ocean with each wave covered the sand as it gradually edged up a little further on the shore. After slowly covering the sand in approximately six hours, the ocean quietly receded back to its depth. The timing is so accurate that the time of the high and low tides twice a day can be told many days in advance.

God created the seas and controls them. Rivers and streams are constantly flowing into the seas, and yet the seas never overflow. They can only go as far as He gives them permission.

"He gave the sea its boundary so the waters would not overstep his command" (Proverbs 8:29).

When Jesus was here on earth, He spoke and the waves became calm.

Then he got into the boat, and his disciples followed Him. Suddenly, a furious storm came up on the lake, so that the waves swept over the boat. But Jesus was sleeping. The disciples went and woke him, saying, "Lord save us! We are going to drown!"

He replied, "You of little faith, why are you so afraid?" Then he got up and rebuked the winds and the waves, and it was completely calm (Matthew 8:23–27).

It is the Lord who causes the wind to force the waves high, giving them power during a storm. He also tells the wind to be still so the waves again become calm, flowing water.

Do you ask and trust the Lord, who controls the wind and waves, to help and give you guidance in the turmoil of your life when you don't know how to react in a situation?

Western Plains

The Lord is my shepherd, I lack nothing. He makes me lie
down in green pastures, he leads me beside quiet waters.

—Psalm 23:1–2

Below the mountains in the north Midwest are miles
and miles of open range with small, rolling hills and
streams. Cattle, bison, horses, and sheep are scattered
with many miles between. Some are in groups, and others are
alone.

These animals may be branded by their owners; but it is
God who created them and owns them. "For every animal of
the forest is mine, and the cattle on a thousand hills" (Psalm
50:10).

Watching a flock of sheep being gathered together to go
to a new pasture reminded me of the tenth chapter of John.
Just as the man gathered and led his sheep to a new pasture,
the Lord, who is the good shepherd and gave His life for you,
wants to care for and lead you in the right direction as you
travel here on earth until He brings you home to Him.

Psalm 23 tells how the Lord, as your shepherd, leads you
through life. He supplies all your needs (Philippians 4:19); He

gives you peace and strength as you need them (Psalm 29:11). He is merciful and forgiving (1 John 1:9) and is beside you when you are facing difficult situations (Deuteronomy 31:6). He surrounds you with His unfailing love (Psalm 32:10) until He calls you home.

Psalm 139:1–4 tells us that the Lord knows all about His sheep, the people that have accepted Christ as their Savior.

Have you accepted the Lord Jesus Christ as your Savior? Are you one of the Lord's sheep?

Reminders

Give ear and come to me; listen, that you may live.
I will make an everlasting covenant with you.
—Isaiah 55:3

Doctors give a card stating the time of your next appointment. You may also receive a call to remind you of the approaching date. At that time, you have the option to keep, postpone, or cancel the appointment.

God is calling you today. "Seek the LORD while he may be found; call on him while he is near" (Isaiah 55:6).

We are told, "God will bring into judgment both the righteous and the wicked, for there will be a time for every activity, a time to judge every deed" (Ecclesiastes 3:17).

Hebrews 9:27 reminds us that people die only once, and then they are judged.

God, in His mercy, has given you His Word, the Bible, to tell how to be ready to meet death. "For God so loved the world that he gave his one and only Son, that whoever believes in him shall not perish but have eternal life" (John 3:16).

Do not to harden your heart by refusing to accept what God is saying. Over a period of time, if you refuse to listen to the Lord calling you, your heart will become hard as concrete, and you will not be able to hear Him calling.

Today is the day of salvation (2 Corinthians 6:2).

Unlike the time of the doctor's appointment, you cannot cancel the day you will pass into eternity.

Are you putting off accepting His invitation today, while He is still calling you?

Chevrolet's Advertisement

He is the Rock, his works are perfect, and
all his ways are just. A faithful God who
does no wrong, upright and just is he.
—Deuteronomy 32:4

In 1991, Chevrolet claimed that their trucks were like a rock. Are they? Many things may go wrong: a flat tire or motor problems.

God is never impaired. God is not only like a rock; He is *the Rock!* To believers, Jesus Christ is the cornerstone; to nonbelievers, He is a stumbling stone (1 Peter 2:6–8).

Everyone is building his or her life on something or someone. It could be the accumulation of wealth, popularity, prestige, or trying to please a particular person. All these things are temporary and can be gone tomorrow. None of these things can be taken into eternity. It is building your life on worthless sand.

There are two choices; building your spiritual house on the rock or on the sand. Matthew 7:24–27 tells you the difference.

Therefore everyone who hears these words of mine and puts them into practice is like a wise man who built his house on the rock. The rain came down, the streams rose, and the winds blew and beat against that house; yet it did not fall, because it had its foundation on the rock. But everyone who hears these words of mine and does not put them into practice is like a foolish man who built his house on sand. The rain came down, the streams rose, and the winds blew and beat against that house, and it fell with a great crash.

Only a life built on Christ, the cornerstone, will endure. Only what is done for Christ while we live will count. God will reward you according to what you have done for Him.

Are you building your life on shifting sand or on the Rock, who is Jesus Christ, the Savior?

Prices

Jesus Christ is the same yesterday and today and forever.
—Hebrews 13:8

P rices often fluctuate from store to store. Discount stores sell the same item for less than specialty shops. On certain days, sales are offered. The same gas company will have different prices at different locations. Prices are not the only things that change. Governments may change their rules to accomplish what they want. What may be politically correct today may be politically incorrect tomorrow. Dress styles change according to the culture of the day. Your own desires may change as you grow older or due to circumstances.

God never changes.

God's laws are the same today as they were in the beginning. The Ten Commandments given to Moses have not changed and still apply. We cannot change them by deleting them or adding to them.

"I know that everything God does will endure forever; nothing can be added to it and nothing taken from it. God does it so that people will fear him" (Ecclesiastes 3:14).

People like to think of God as only a God of love. He is a God of love, but also a holy and just God. The promises of God do not change. If you love and obey God, He will bless you.

He will correct you when you disobey Him, or wander away from Him, because He loves you and wants you to have a close relationship with Him.

"My son, do not despise the LORD's discipline, and do not resent his rebuke, because the LORD disciplines those he loves, as a father the son he delights in" (Proverbs 3:11–12).

Are you leaning on the everlasting God who never changes?

The Wind

The fool says in his heart, "There is no God."
—Psalm 14:1

A person cannot see the wind. Only the wind's effect can be seen and felt by everyone and everything as it passes.

Just as we cannot see the wind, only feel its effects, the same is true with God. He cannot be seen, but His presence can be felt.

I was attending my sister's church a month after my husband died when the feeling of Bill's absence was too much for me. I didn't want to cry in front of strangers. As I sat fighting the tears that were slowly running down my face, I felt two arms slowly sliding down my arms, warming me and giving me comfort. I no longer felt alone. My tears stopped. I knew God was with me.

When your thoughts are focused on God, you can feel His presence through the peace He gives you when you are upset. "You will keep in perfect peace those whose minds are steadfast, because they trust in you" (Isaiah 26:3).

When you feel as if you cannot take another step, it is God who gives you the strength and staying power to keep going. "It is God who arms me with strength and keeps my way secure" (Psalm 18:32).

If you ask, God will give you the wisdom you need in all situations (Proverbs 2:6). He will also help you to think twice before you say words you will regret when you ask Him to set a guard over your mouth (Psalm 141:3).

God was with you before you were born. He surrounds you wherever you are. He knows all you will think say or do before you do. He surrounds you constantly (Psalm 139).

Remember, even though you cannot see God, you can feel His presence.

Snow

"Come now, and let us settle the matter," says
the LORD. "Though your sins are like scarlet,
they shall be as white as snow; though they are
red as crimson, they shall be like wool."
—Isaiah 1:18

Watching the snow descending, like a great, white blanket, covering all it touched, made me think of the above verse.

As the snow covers everything, making it spotless, Jesus Christ's death on the cross covers all our sin, making us spotless before God (Colossians 1:22).

"Therefore, if any man be in Christ, he is a new creation; old things are passed away; behold, all things are become new" (2 Corinthians 5:17 KJV).

Sin separates a person from God. Therefore, God provided the way for a relationship with Him by having His Son, Jesus Christ, pay the penalty for our sin by His death on Calvary's cross.

A person needs to acknowledge he or she is a sinner and accept Jesus' death on the cross as the only payment needed for all his or her past, present, and future sins.

There are not enough good deeds, enough money, or prayers long enough to cover sin. Salvation is a free gift to everyone who believes and accepts Jesus Christ as Savior and Lord.

"For it is by grace you have been saved, through faith—and this is not from yourselves, it is the gift of God—not by works, so that no one can boast" (Ephesians 2:8–9).

Trust Him when Jesus Christ says that whoever believes on Him will not be condemned. "Therefore, there is now no condemnation for those who are in Christ Jesus, because through Christ Jesus the law of the Spirit who gives life has set you free from the law of sin and death" (Romans 8:1-2).

Have you accepted Jesus Christ as your Savior, that He may present you spotless before God?

Soap

But when the kindness and the love of God our Savior appeared, he saved us, not because of righteous things we had done, but because of his mercy. He saved us through the washing of rebirth and renewal by the Holy Spirit, whom he poured out on us generously through Jesus Christ our Savior.
—Titus 3:4–6

The advertisement says, "Use Dial soap and get rid of bacteria and germs." Another advertisement says, "If you want soap for all your two thousand parts, use Lever soap."

As good as these soaps may be, they are useless sitting on the closet shelf or when used without adding water. Adding water makes the lather, and the more water that is added, the more lather a person has. It is the lather that gets your physical body clean.

You also need the water of the Word of God and the help of the Holy Spirit to help you keep your spiritual life clean. The more you lean on the Holy Spirit to help and guide you, the more you will become the person God knows you can be.

"Wash and make yourselves clean. Take your evil deeds out of my sight; stop doing wrong" (Isaiah 1:16).

The Holy Spirit wants to fill every area of your life to help strengthen you to live a life that is honoring to the Lord. He will help you when you pray and remind you what the Lord has said.

As the Holy Spirit convicts you of your sin, confess it to the Lord and He will forgive you. God will not refuse anyone who comes humbly to Him for forgiveness believing that Christ died for that person.

"Therefore, since we have these promises, dear friends, let us purify ourselves from everything that contaminates body and spirit, perfecting holiness out of reverence for God" (2 Corinthians 7:1).

Will you take your Bible off the shelf and allow the Holy Spirit guide you as you read it daily for cleansing and guidance?

Expiration Date

So, as the Holy Spirit says: Today, if you hear his voice,
do not harden your hearts as you did in the rebellion."
—Hebrews 3:7–8

I t is the law to put the expiration date on food and medicine. This is the last date that the product should be used before losing its freshness or medicinal value.

You also have an expiration date. While you are living, God gives you time and opportunities to accept His invitation to come to Him.

"The Spirit and the bride say, 'Come!' And let the one who hears say, 'Come!' Let the one who is thirsty come; and let the one who wishes take the free gift of the water of life" (Revelation 22:17).

You do not know what will happen tomorrow; therefore, ask yourself, is it worth clinging to whatever is hindering you from accepting God's free gift of salvation?

"What good is it for someone to gain the whole world, yet forfeit their soul? Or what can anyone give in exchange for their soul?" (Mark 8:36–37).

You can have the assurance of eternal life. "Praise be to the God and Father of our Lord Jesus Christ! In His great mercy He has given us new birth into a living hope through the resurrection of Jesus Christ from the dead, and into an inheritance that can never perish, spoil or fade. This inheritance is kept in heaven for you" (1 Peter 1:3–4).

Once your life is over on earth, the time for your choice to accept Christ as Savior and Lord of your life has expired.

Have you accepted God's invitation for eternal life with Him?

CAPD

Blessed is the one who does not walk in step with the wicked or stand in the way that sinners take or sit in the company of mockers, but whose delight is in the law of the LORD, and who meditates on his law day and night.
—Psalm 1:1–2

Continuous Ambulatory Peritoneal Dialysis (CAPD) has three functions: filling, dwelling, and draining. The medicated solution enters through a shunt into the peritoneum. After four to six hours, it is drained, taking all the impurities out of the body. It is replaced with new medicated solution. The exchange needs repeating four times a day, every day.

To follow Christ, you need to follow a similar routine. You need to fill your mind with the truth of the Word of God and dwell, or meditate, on what you read. Ask, "What does it mean? How can I apply it daily in my actions and reactions?"

Like CAPD, you need to exchange your willful thoughts with thoughts of Christ. You can choose what you allow your mind to dwell on. You can think of the positive or the negative. It is your choice on what you dwell.

"Finally, brothers and sisters, whatever is true, whatever is noble, whatever is right, whatever is pure, whatever is lovely, whatever is admirable—if anything is excellent or praiseworthy—think about such things" (Philippians 4:8).

May you say, "I have hidden your word in my heart that I might not sin against you" (Psalm 119:11).

Are your thoughts dwelling on God's Word?

"Turn your eyes upon Jesus,
look full in His wonderful face;
and the things of earth will grow strangely dim
in the light of His glory and grace."

Bible Verses

But the Advocate, the Holy Spirit, whom the Father
will send in my name, will teach you all things and
will remind you of everything I have said to you.
—John 14:26

The Lord promised that the Holy Spirit would help you to pray and to remember everything the Lord has said to help you in your life experiences and conversations. But how can you recall what the Lord has said if you have not memorized Bible verses?

God has given you many verses in the book of Psalms where you can find words of comfort (119:50), of hope (71:5), of mercy (51:1), of peace (4:8).

There are verses explaining what your attitude and behavior should be. You should love your enemies, do good, be merciful, be forgiving, and be givers. You are not to judge or to condemn anyone (Colossians 3:12–14).

There are verses to help you during your roughest days. You are told that God is with you as your helper and comforter (Hebrews 13:6). He is able to defend and protect you (Deuteronomy 10:18). He watches over you and supplies all that you need (Philippians 4:19). He will forgive you when you ask Him (Psalm 86:5). When grieving, you are told, "Do not grieve, for the joy of the LORD is your strength" (Nehemiah 8:10).

Are you memorizing Bible verses?

God Is Always with You

Starting each day
Opening your heart in prayer (Psalm 5:3),

Reading God's Word
Saying you are never alone (Hebrews 13:5),

God is your helper (Hebrews 13:6).
He is your defender (Deuteronomy 10:18).

God watches over you;
He guides you with His eye (Psalm 32:8).
All your needs He supplies (Philippians 4:19).

With His protecting arm,
He holds you close (Isaiah 43:2)
When walking in the way of harm.

He holds your hand,
Helping you walk (Psalm 139:9–10)
Through His plan.

When you are grieving,
You find your strength in the joy of the Lord (Nehemiah 8:10).

At the end of each day,
With a thankful heart,
May you always pray:

"Heavenly Father, thank you
For being with me today (Isaiah 46:4),
For your words of comfort,

For your forgiveness
For saying what I should not have said (1 John 1:9),
For not saying what I should."

Preparing a Garden

I, the LORD search the heart and examine the
mind, to reward each person according to their
conduct, according to what their deeds deserve.
—Jeremiah 17:10

A garden needs constant work to be productive. The
ground needs to be cultivated and fertilized for
nourishment before seeds can be planted. To prevent
the soil from becoming dry or baked by the sun, daily watering
is necessary. Weeds need to be removed before their roots grow
too deep.

Your mind is like a garden. Just as you decide what to plant
in your garden, you need to decide on which thoughts you
will dwell and whom you will believe. You are not to believe
anyone who preaches that Jesus Christ is not the Son of God
(1 John 4:1-3).

As you need to water the garden to help your plants grow,
your nourishment to grow spiritually needs to come through
meditating on what you read in the Bible and through prayer.
You need to put into action what you read.

Are you cultivating your mind as Philippians 4:8 says? "Finally, brothers and sisters, whatever is true, whatever is noble, whatever is right, whatever is pure, whatever is lovely, whatever is admirable—if anything is excellent or praiseworthy—think about such things."

When you ask the Holy Spirit, He will reveal your wrong thoughts and attitudes. You must choose to remove them, as you would remove weeds from a garden. Like weeds, you need to remove them promptly. The longer the wrong thoughts and attitudes stay in your mind, the harder it is to get rid of them.

Ask the Lord, "Test me, LORD, and try me, examine my heart and my mind" (Psalm 26:2).

Are you willing to remove the wrong thoughts and replace them with thoughts of thanksgiving and praise honoring God?

Ear of Corn

No one serving as a soldier gets entangled in civilian affairs,
but rather tries to please his commanding officer. Similarly,
anyone who competes as an athlete does not receive the
victor's crown except by competing according to the rules.

—2 Timothy 2:4–5

Before an ear of corn can be eaten, the outer leaves and silken strands need to be removed.

It is the same in your spiritual life. The outer leaves are pride and self-sufficiency. The silken strands that are entwined into the kernels are the old wrong habits that are often hard to correct or stop.

As a soldier of Jesus Christ, you should not let secular desires overrule what you know Jesus Christ wants you to do. You need to obey Him and submit yourself to Him.

A runner in a race does not carry more than he needs. He doesn't want any extra weight that prevents him from winning. He also keeps his eyes focused on the goal.

You, also, need to let go of anything that is hindering you from having a close relationship with the Lord. He wants to help you to be all He knows you can be. As soon as you start to travel in the wrong direction, you need to say, "Stop!"

Ask the Lord to refocus your actions and to close your eyes from looking at things that are not worth anything (Psalm 119:37).

"Therefore, since we are surrounded by such a great cloud of witnesses, let us throw off everything that hinders and the sin that so easily entangles. And let us run with perseverance the race marked out for us" (Hebrews 12:1).

Are you getting rid of whatever is hindering you from completing the race that God has called you to run?

Beauty Salon

He has made us competent as ministers of the
new covenant—not of the letter but of the Spirit;
for the letter kills, but the Spirit gives life.
—2 Corinthians 3:6

Sitting in a beauty salon watching the women getting their hair colored, trimmed and styled, or in some cases getting a permanent, to get the results that they desired reminded me that the Lord uses different methods to help a person to grow spiritually.

Whatever else you're having done, your hair must be washed first.

As your hair needs to be washed first, your first need is to accept Christ as your Savior. You need to believe and accept that His death on the cross is the only way for your sins to be forgiven.

Having your hair trimmed is similar to the Lord showing what needs to be removed from your life.

Permanents and hair coloring take longer to complete. Individual attention must be given in the selection of the product used, the process, and the timing. For a permanent to be successful, only certain chemicals can be used. The length of time varies with the different textures of hair and the tightness of the curls. Just as those factors affect the time needed for a permanent to be accomplished, the person's willingness to listen to God will affect how fast that person will grow spiritually. It is not done by using chemicals but through studying God's Word and following through on what you read.

The Lord will use the best method and the length of time He knows is necessary to mold and shape your heart and mind to conform to His likeness and for you to be willing to fulfill what He wants you to accomplish for His glory.

He will use the process that will get your attention. God created each person differently, and He knows the correct process for each person.

Are you letting the Lord mold your heart and mind to be conformed to His image and to do His will in your life?

Unfinished Tablecloth

Being confident of this, that he who began
a good work in you will carry it on to
completion until the day of Christ Jesus.
—Philippians 1:6

When my granddaughter became engaged, she asked me to crochet a tablecloth for her.

At the time of the bridal shower, I gave my granddaughter the half-finished tablecloth. She proudly held it up, saying, "My grandmother is in the process of finishing this tablecloth for me."

As my granddaughter knew I would finish the tablecloth, we know God will finish His work in us. Christ and the Holy Spirit want to work in your life to present you to the Father without fault.

"To him who is able to keep you from stumbling and to present you before his glorious presence without fault and with great joy" (Jude 24).

God sent the Holy Spirit to guide and help you. You are given a free will. You need to decide how much you let the

Holy Spirit rule in your thoughts and actions. He will not force Himself.

In the finishing process, the Lord may use discipline. Then we should ask, "What am I doing or thinking that is displeasing to the Lord? What does the Lord want me to do?" When you are told what is wrong in your actions or conversations, ask the Lord for forgiveness and to help you change your lifestyle.

God works in you and through you as you choose to submit to Him. Do not resist His corrections. You will be the loser.

Philippians 2:13 tells you that "For it is God who works in you to will and to act in order to fulfill his good purpose."

Are your mind and heart open to accept God's chiding and leading so that you will be made complete in Him?

Patterns

Now that I, your Lord and Teacher, have washed your feet,
you also should wash one another's feet. I have set you
an example that you should do as I have done for you.
—John 13:14–15

In knitting or crocheting, you choose a particular pattern. Instructions are given as to the size of needles or hook, and also the type of yarn. In sewing, the pattern has directions as to how the pattern pieces are to be laid on the material and where to sew the seams. These instructions are given to insure the correct results.

While Jesus Christ was here on earth, His lifestyle showed us the pattern we are to follow so we will grow to be more like Him. He was humble (Philippians 2:8), forgiving, and gracious (Luke 4:22). He did not show partiality. He healed both the rich and the poor (Matthew 9:18–25). He ate with important and unimportant people (Mark 2:15).

Jesus asked His Father to forgive the people for what they were doing while He was hanging on the cross (Luke 23:34). In the sample prayer Jesus gave us, we are to ask to be forgiven as we have forgiven others. Jesus then explains that if you do not forgive people, God will not forgive you (Matthew 6:9-15).

Everything Jesus did He did with compassion and love. You are to show love in your conversations, actions, and reactions.

"In everything set them an example by doing what is good. In your teaching show integrity, seriousness, and soundness of speech that cannot be condemned, so that those who oppose you may be ashamed because they have nothing bad to say about us" (Titus 2:7).

Does the pattern of your life reflect the love of God?

Climbing a Ladder

But grow in the grace and knowledge of
our Lord and Savior Jesus Christ.
—2 Peter 3:18

To climb a ladder, you need to put your foot on the first rung and your other foot on the next rung; then you continue putting a foot on one rung at a time until you reach the top. It takes desire, determination, and strength to continue climbing.

The Christian life is similar to climbing a ladder. The first rung of the spiritual ladder is accepting Christ as your Savior.

"Jesus answered, 'I am the way and the truth and the life. No one comes to the Father except through me'" (John 14:6).

Starting the climb up the ladder, you need the desire to read the Bible to learn what God is telling you so you will grow spiritually (1 Peter 2:2). Also, a quiet time is needed to be spent in prayer talking to God and waiting with patience to listen for His answer.

Remembering the faithfulness of God and His help in the past helps you to have the determination to grow spiritually.

You climb a ladder one rung at a time to reach what you want. On your spiritual ladder, seek after righteousness and godliness. You also need to grow in faith, in love, in patience, and in gentleness (1 Timothy 6:11).

God will give you strength when you need it. Ask Him to help you every step along the way (Hebrews 4:16).

Are you growing in knowledge and faith on your spiritual ladder?

Rosebush

Jesus answered, "Very truly I tell you, no
one can enter the kingdom of God unless
they are born of water and the Spirit."
—John 3:5

My rosebush was blooming with many beautiful red roses. Then weeks of clear, hot, dry, sunny days caused the leaves to wilt and the roses to die. When the rain again came softly and steadily, the rosebush revived. Green leaves reappeared, and the bush boasted beautiful red roses.

Like the rosebush, your walk with the Lord will become dry and barren if you neglect the necessary living water of the Word of God. You must allow it to sink steadily into your heart to bring forth fruit in your life.

Galatians 5:16 says, "So I say, walk by the Spirit, and you will not gratify the desires of the flesh."

Spending quiet and quality time in studying and meditating on the scriptures is necessary to grow spiritually and to become more like Jesus Christ.

When you do, you will reap the fruit of the Spirit, which is love, joy, peace, forbearance, kindness, goodness, faithfulness, gentleness, and self-control (Galatians 5:22).

As you study God's Word, ask yourself, "What is God telling me, and how does this apply to me?" Follow through on what you have been told.

If your relationship with the Lord is barren, will you begin to study His Word, pray, and obey His will so your relationship with Him will revive and grow?

Knowledge

The fear of the Lord is the beginning of knowledge,
but fools despise wisdom and instruction.
—Proverbs 1:7

CNBC News 10 states, "Knowledge is power." Yes, knowledge is powerful and important. It has been used for good and for evil.

As you gather knowledge to help in your secular life, it is just as important to gather knowledge from God's Word for your spiritual life and to find God's will for you.

Lessons are learned and tests in school are passed by memorizing facts and figures. Also, when you memorize scripture verses, God will bring to your memory the exact verse when you need it.

A smart man will learn all he needs to know to be better equipped to advance in his vocation. A wise man will study the scriptures to learn all he can about God's laws and promises. He will learn to discern which promises God gives unconditionally and which promises have conditions. Some promises have conditions to be followed before they can be fulfilled.

"Instruct the wise and they will be wiser still; teach the righteous and they will add to their learning" (Proverbs 9:9).

A wise man will heed God's instructions on how his life should be lived. He is to be faithful, gentle, and forgiving; he is to have patience and self-control. Actions speak louder than words. Be sure your lifestyle matches your words.

"Apply your heart to instruction and your ears to words of knowledge" (Proverbs 23:12).

Are you increasing your knowledge of the scriptures? Are you living according to your knowledge?

Light Bulb

You are the light of the world. A town built on a hill
cannot be hidden. Neither do people light a lamp and
put it under a bowl. Instead they put it on its stand,
and it gives light to everyone in the house. In the same
way, let your light shine before others, that they may see
your good deeds and glorify your Father in heaven.
—Matthew 5:14–16

When day turns to night, we need a light to see. It
is not enough to hold a lamp. The lamp needs
to be connected to an outside power and turned
on. To be a light for Jesus Christ, you need to be connected
daily to the LORD, for He is the power that makes your light
shine. To be connected, you need to believe that Jesus Christ
is the Son of God and that He died on Calvary's cross to pay
the penalty for your sins.

Before accepting Jesus Christ as your Savior, you were in
darkness. After accepting Jesus Christ as your Savior, you are
a light in the Lord. You are to live as a child of light, showing
goodness, forgiveness, righteousness, and truth. You should

now live a life pleasing to the Lord and not a life that reflects your former way of pleasing only yourself.

"Not that we are competent in ourselves to claim anything for ourselves, but our competence comes from God" (2 Corinthians 3:5).

To walk as a child of light, you need to have a close relationship with Christ. To keep that close relationship, you need to pray and read your Bible. Ask the Holy Spirit to help you understand what you read and to show you where you have sinned so you can ask to be forgiven and have your relationship with Him restored.

May you say, "Your word is a lamp to my feet, a light on my path" (Psalm 119:105).

Does your life reflect Christ in your life?

Fishing

"Come, follow me," Jesus said, "and I will
send you out to fish for people."
—Matthew 4:19

Over the years, I have learned there is more to fishing than just putting a line, hook, bait, and a lead weight in the water. There are many important facts to remember. It takes patience and perseverance. You must learn to fish in the right place and at the right time. You need to know the right size hook and the correct bait for the type of fish you want to catch.

Apply this to "fishing for men." The first preparation step is knowing what the Bible says and persevering in prayer. It is necessary to keep alert, looking for the opportunity to speak and asking the Holy Spirit to give you the right words and expression as you talk. It is not just what is said, but the way it is said.

You are to be like Paul, who made himself be a servant and put himself in the place of everyone he was telling about Christ, who paid the debt for their sins.

"How, then, can they call on the one they have not believed in? And how can they believe in the one of whom they have not heard? And how can they hear without someone preaching to them?" (Romans 10:14).

Encourage the person to accept Christ as Savior and not to put off his or her decision. Tomorrow may be too late. No one knows what will happen the next day.

"Now listen, you who say, 'Today or tomorrow we will go to this or that city, spend a year there, carry on business and make money.' Why, you do not even know what will happen tomorrow" (James 4:13–14).

Are you using every opportunity to tell other people of Christ's love for them and the only way of salvation?

Applied Heat

Let no debt remain outstanding, except the continuing
debt to love one another, for whoever loves others has
fulfilled the law. Love does no harm to a neighbor.
Therefore, love is the fulfillment of the law.
—Romans 13:8, 10

For thirty minutes, the plumber persistently used a chisel and a hammer, trying to separate two metal pipes that were stuck together. Realizing he was only putting dents in the pipe and not making any progress, the plumber decided to use an acetylene torch.

The heat was evenly applied all around the outer pipe several times. The heat slowly loosened the outer pipe, and the two pipes were easily separated.

"Dear children, let us not love with words or speech but with actions and in truth" (1 John 3:18).

Using the acetylene torch to apply the heat around the pipes is the same as showing Jesus Christ's love to those around you. You show His love for people by willingly helping physically when needed and showing that you care with a hug, smile, or listening ear.

Your caring actions, reactions, and attitudes may give others the desire to have Christ in their lives and to separate themselves from the enticements of the world.

You may be the only example of Christ and His love that a person may ever see.

Are your actions reflecting the love of Christ?

Extra Quarters

Command them to do good, to be rich in good
deeds, and to be generous and willing to share.
—1 Timothy 6:18

I had only a ten-dollar bill, but I knew the Laundromat had a coin machine. When I arrived, another customer told me the coin machine was broken. He offered me a five-dollar bill and five singles to get change from the coin machine in the post office next door.

In my haste, I put the five-dollar bill in the slot for stamps. Now I only had enough change to wash but not to dry my laundry.

A friend came in, and when I told her what had happened, she generously gave me plenty of quarters. Another customer entered who did not have enough quarters. I gladly gave her the extra quarters that I did not need.

The Lord often gives you more than you need so you can help others. When you have the opportunity, help someone with a smile and a willing heart. The amount you give, or what you do, does not matter, but the thought and the way it is given does matter. Many times, it is not material things that are needed as much as a phone call, a listening ear, or a visit.

You also please God when you share what you have with a willing heart, for God loves a cheerful giver. You are God's hands and feet to help others.

When you are able, you are to give freely and cheerfully. "If anyone has material possessions and sees a brother or sister in need but has no pity on them, how can the love of God be in that person?" (1 John 3:17).

Are you helping others from the abundance that the Lord has given you?

A Broken Hand

Just as the body, though one, has many parts, but all
its many parts form one body, so it is with Christ.
If one part suffers, every part suffers with it; if one
part is honored, every part rejoices with it.
—1 Corinthians 12:12, 26

The right and left hands often work together. If one
hand is incapacitated, it will affect what a person
can do unassisted. Many jobs would be left undone
or take twice the time to complete with only one functional
hand. At that time, a person may need to ask for help.

If one hand is unusable, a person needs to use the chest
and an arm to hold anything heavy. The mouth may be used
as a substitute for carrying parcels. If a leg is hurt, crutches
may be needed. Blindness requires sensitive fingers and alert,
hearing ears. Each part of the human body has a function that
only it can do.

How like the family of God. God has given His children
different personalities and gifts to help and strengthen each
other (Ephesians 4:11–16).

God gives wisdom, knowledge, and faith, enabling a person to show others the way of salvation. Also given is the ability to discern when a person is not preaching that Jesus Christ is the Son of God. One gift that everyone has been given is the power and ability to pray for one another (1 Samuel 12:23).

You should not wish to have some other person's gift. "But in fact God has placed the parts in the body, every one of them, just as he wanted them to be" (1 Corinthians 12:18).

If one member is not using the gift that God has given him or her to help when needed, the whole church family will suffer.

Also, if you do not listen to the Lord and do what He has asked you to do, He may ask someone else, and that person will get the blessing the Lord intended for you.

Are you fulfilling your part in your church family?

Seventy-Five Cents

The blessing of the LORD brings wealth,
without painful toil for it.
—Proverbs 10:22

In a store, a happy young boy once said, "I'm rich." He had seventy-five cents left after his purchase. Someone else might consider that to be only pocket change. No matter a person's status in life, rich or poor, famous or unknown, if that person is having a close relationship with the Lord, he or she is rich.

Yes, money is necessary and does buy tangible items. For a short period, you have pleasure in what you bought. Outside influences and circumstances also can give temporary happiness.

But the blessings and wealth of the Lord are lasting. Your sins are forgiven. You cannot pay the debt for your sins; only Jesus Christ could, and He did by dying on the cross for you.

"In him we have redemption through his blood, the forgiveness of sins, in accordance with the riches of God's grace" (Ephesians 1:7).

If you have a close relationship with the Lord, you have hope (Jeremiah 17:7), joy (Nehemiah 8:10), strength, and inner peace. "The LORD gives strength to his people; the LORD blesses his people with peace" (Psalm 29:11).

Only God can give you peace in the midst of turmoil. These are gifts only He can give, and these gifts cannot be bought or taken away from you.

When you are trusting in God and waiting for His answer, you are never disappointed. If God answers no, either He has something better for you or it is not the right time to receive it.

Joy in the Lord is knowing that your sins are forgiven by believing and accepting Christ's death on the cross as payment for our sins. It is a free gift.

Even in trials, you can have the joy of the Lord, knowing that He is able to help you through it. Your joy is not dependent on what you do for the Lord but on your obeying Him. Joy in the Lord is expecting His good for you in all situations of life.

Are you enjoying the riches of God in Christ Jesus?

Election

Whoever believes in him is not condemned, but whoever does not believe stands condemned already because they have not believed in the name of God's one and only Son.
—John 3:18

The first Tuesday in November is Election Day. On that day, you have a choice to vote or not to vote to select whom you want in the many different positions to lead your city, state, or country.

There is a much more important decision you need to make. It is personal, and only you can cast your vote. No one can make it for you. You have no other options. You have to choose between Christ and Satan. This choice should be made today, for no one knows what will happen, and tomorrow may be too late.

"Do not boast about tomorrow, for you do not know what a day may bring" (Proverbs 27:1).

The decision you make will affect where you will spend eternity. Believing in Jesus Christ will guarantee that you will have eternal life and that you will be spending eternity in heaven with Him.

"Whoever believes in the Son has eternal life, but whoever rejects the Son will not see life, for God's wrath remains on them" (John 3:36).

You are warned that the devil is the father of lies (John 8:44); he is the ruler of darkness (Ephesians 6:12), and he wants to trap you (2 Timothy 2:26).

Jesus Christ is the truth (John 1:14); He rules in light (1 John 1:5), and He will set you free (Galatians 5:1).

Before it is too late, come to Jesus Christ. He is waiting to welcome you. Resist the devil, and he will run away from you (James 4:7–8).

Jesus Christ is inviting you to come to Him and have eternal life. "I, even I, am he who blots out your transgressions, for my sake, and remembers your sins no more" (Isaiah 43:25).

Will you elect to accept Jesus Christ as your Lord?

Bubbles

Therefore, dear friends, since you have been forewarned,
be on your guard so that you may not be carried away by
the error of the lawless and fall from your secure position.

—2 Peter 3:17

Watching the bubbles slowly go down the drain
caused me to think of the parable of the soils
(Luke 8). The bubbles floating freely in the
middle were the first to go. Then the bubbles floating near
the side of the bowl were the next to slowly disappear. But
the bubbles attached to the bowl's side had to be wiped away.

The freely floating bubbles reminded me of the people
who do not have any desire to know Christ. They go along
with the world's concept that "all roads lead to God" or it is
okay "pleasing only themselves."

The bubbles floating near the side of the bowl reminded
me of the people who heard about Christ's love and accepted
Him as Savior but were discouraged or became entangled
with the cares of this world or decided to follow the crowd,
succumbing to peer pressure.

The bubbles clinging to the side of the bowl reminded me of the people who lean on God by studying His Word, obeying His commands and clinging to Him. Therefore, Satan has a harder time persuading them to go with the flow.

"Trust in the LORD with all your heart and lean not on your own understanding; in all your ways submit to him, and he will make your paths straight" (Proverbs 3:5–6).

"Submit yourselves, then, to God. Resist the devil, and he will flee from you" (James 4:7).

Are you swayed by the forces of the world, or are you standing strong on the Word of God?

Misplaced Ring

Do not be far from me, my God; come
quickly, God, to help me.
—Psalm 71:12

After my husband died, I looked for his diamond ring to fulfill his request that each daughter would get one diamond. All I remembered was holding it in my hand just before the casket was closed.

There was only one thing to do. Search! I searched all the drawers and closets. They were cleaned and straightened from the kitchen to the bedrooms.

Not finding the ring, I told God I needed that ring and when I wanted it. His answer was Psalm 46:10: "He says, 'Be still, and know that I am God.'"

I would wake up at night, toss and turn, and tell God that the ring was not mine—it belonged to my daughters. Again, God gave me the same answer.

I told God I could turn in a claim to the insurance company and get the money, but that would not replace the ring. If I found the ring, I would return the money. Also, I told

God I was sorry I had given Bill's clothes away because I was not able to recheck the pockets a third time.

Waking up in the middle of the night, I told God again that I needed to find that ring and when it had to be found. For the third time, He gave me the same answer. When I did not listen and kept asking, there were no more answers.

Was God testing my faith? Was it because I was thinking of my ego, wanting to show the insurance company I was honest? Was it that I did not believe His answer, or my regretting doing what I knew God wanted me to do with Bill's clothes?

Finally, I realized I needed to change my prayer. I told God that I knew He knew where the ring was and asked Him to please show me when He was ready. This time, I did not scheme or plan what to tell my daughters.

It took eight months of prayer before God answered and the ring was found.

Do you wait patiently for God to answer your prayer according to His timing and His will?

Chorus

Be strong and courageous. Do not be afraid or terrified
because of them, for the LORD your God goes with
you; he will never leave you nor forsake you.
—Deuteronomy 31:6

"Just a closer walk with thee.
Grant it, Jesus, is my plea.
Daily walking close to thee.
Let it be, Lord, let it be."

The above is the chorus of a well-known hymn. As I
sang, it came to me that I am sure Jesus is saying to
everyone, "Abide in me."

Jesus does not leave us (Hebrews 13:5). He promised to be
with us all the time. We often forget Him when our lives are
going smoothly without any problems, or when the pleasures
of the world entice us and we leave him.

God did not make us to be puppets to obey when strings
are pulled. He gave us a free will to choose willingly with
whom we want to spend time.

"So then, just as you received Christ Jesus as Lord, continue to live your lives in him, rooted and built up in him, strengthened in the faith as you were taught, and overflowing with thankfulness" (Colossians 2:6–7).

Jesus desires for you to walk close to Him. He asks you to let Him carry your burdens. Only He can give you peace and the rest you need.

"Come to me, all you who are weary and burdened, and I will give you rest. Take my yoke upon you and learn from me, for I am gentle and humble in heart, and you will find rest for your souls. For my yoke is easy and my burden is light" (Matthew 11:28–30).

Are you letting a busy routine and the love of this world come between you and Jesus Christ?

Telephone

For the eyes of the Lord are on the righteous and
his ears are attentive to their prayer, but the face
of the Lord is against those who do evil.
—1 Peter 3:12

When calling someone, you hope the other person will answer. It is disheartening hearing the phone ringing with no answer or getting a recording asking you to leave your name and a brief message. The busy signal can also be frustrating as you dial again and again.

Doubting God will answer your prayer is the same as not getting an answer when telephoning someone. God requires faith on your part for your prayer to be answered (James 1:6–7).

Another reason God is not answering may be that there is something in your life stopping the answer. Ask God to show you what you are doing wrong or the attitudes that should not be in your life. Also ask God to help you overcome them.

"Surely the arm of the Lord is not too short to save, nor his ear too dull to hear. But your iniquities have separated you from your God; your sins have hidden his face from you, so he will not hear" (Isaiah 59:1–2).

Busy signals remind me of when I asked God to help me. He gave me the answer. I did not listen. The next two times I prayed, I received the same answer. After that, God was silent. We need to listen to God's answers and believe what He is telling us.

God knows what the future will be. He will answer your prayer at the right time and when it is for your best.

Are you praying for God's will in your life and for Him to be glorified?

Prayer

Prayer is a two-way conversation,
Talking to God and listening for His response.
It may be yes, no, or even wait.
God is always on time, never late.

Prayer is the most powerful tool
Seldom used as a first recourse.
It is after this or that is done
You remember God is able to overcome.

Answered prayer requires faith,
A steady faith, a faith not wavering.
Praying what is done is God's will.
Knowing this, your heart will be still.

Waiting for God's answer
May be the testing of your faith,
Or God may have a better plan
That will be done, soon as it can.

No answer? Can the reason be
A sin not confessed?
Preventing God to grant your request,
Or doing for you what is best?

Sheepdogs

Let a man so consider us, as servants of Christ
and stewards of the mysteries of God.
—1 Corinthians 4:1 NKJV

Watching the demonstration of a shepherd working his dogs made me ask myself, "Which dog do I represent?"

The owner of the sheep had the one dog bring the sheep to him and then had the other dog scatter the sheep. As he did this, he admitted that the sheep were confused.

Unlike the sheep's owner, the Lord does not confuse His sheep. He does not send anyone away (John 6:37). The Lord invites people to come to Him and have a close relationship with Him (Matthew 11:28).

But as a Christian, which dog do you represent?

Is your lifestyle consistent with the fruit of the Spirit (Galatians 5:22–23)? Do you show love, gentleness, and kindness to others? Do you use self-control or vent your anger? Are you faithful to Jesus Christ?

Or are both dogs being shown in your life by sending conflicting messages by your actions and reactions—one day living a life pleasing to God and the next day enjoying the world's pleasures?

May we pray, "Lord, the LORD Almighty, may those who hope in you not be disgraced because of me; God of Israel, may those who seek you not be put to shame because of me" (Psalm 69:6).

Is your walk matching your talk?

Traveling

I will instruct you and teach you in the way you should
go; I will counsel you with my loving eye on you.
—Psalm 32:8

In great anticipation, my husband and I followed the
directions we had been given to visit our daughter. In the
beginning, the directions were easy to follow. Then we
came to curving roads that appeared to be endless without a
sign showing where we were.

A sign at last! We were on the right road.

We came to an intersection with numerous different road
signs. Which one to take? Looking at the directions, we chose
the correct road. We did not stop while going through the
different towns but were careful to stay on the correct road.

After hours of driving, we were on the last main highway.
It was one of many Vermont roads with a few scattered houses
here and there and then trees and more trees. At last, we saw
a sign giving the name of our daughter's town. Drove for a
few miles and didn't see the street where we were to turn left.

We decided to call and explain where we were by what we
were passing. We also asked how much further it was to her

home. The answer was encouraging. We only had to go a few more miles.

The trip made me realize a Christian life's travel is the same. When you first accept Christ as your Savior, you are enthusiastic about being a follower of Christ.

However, there may be monotonous days and days of trials and disappointments. On these days, God may encourage you by a friend's conversation or by a Bible verse.

The times when you need to make decisions in vocation or friends are the intersections in life. God is ready to help you make the right decision.

Going through towns is similar to the many temptations that come into your life. Keep your eyes on Christ. He is able to help you refuse them.

Calling our daughter to tell her where we were and ask how much further we had to drive is the same as telling God what we feel and asking Him for help in times of trials or uncertainty.

Psalm 37 gives us basic facts to observe and to obey.

Verse 3: "Trust in the Lord and do good."

Verse 4: "Take delight in the Lord."

Verse 5: "Commit your way to the Lord, trust in him."

Verse 7: "Be still before the Lord, and wait patiently for him."

Verse 8: "Refrain from anger, and turn from wrath."

Verse 27: "Turn from evil and do good."

Verse 34: "Hope in the Lord, and keep his way."

Are you listening to God? Are you following His guidelines for your life?

Lost

You have searched me, LORD, and you know me. You
know when I sit and when I rise; you perceive my
thoughts from afar. You discern my going out and
my lying down; you are familiar with all my ways.
—Psalm 139:1–3

While sitting in our boat in the middle of the
Delaware Bay, unable to see land, I wondered
where we were and which way was the correct
direction to go home. After looking at the GPS (Global
Positioning System), I knew where we were, and I knew it
would guide us home.

I thought of the above verse and how wonderful it is that
God knows where I am physically and spiritually and yet
loves me.

The GPS will guide you home when you put in the correct
coordinates. Spiritually, it is the same. God has given you a
GPS, the Bible, for guidance and instruction.

The first coordinate is acknowledging that you are a sinner
and that only accepting Christ's death on the cross paying the
penalty of your sins will lead you to spend eternity with Christ.

The next coordinate is taking time to study God's Word, praying and doing what God tells you.

After putting in the correct coordinates, you trust the GPS to take you in the right direction. You need to trust God and follow the way He is leading you.

"For this God is our God forever and ever; he will be our guide even to the end" (Psalm 48:14).

While following the GPS, you need to be careful as you maneuver your boat through the water, watching for any obstacle floating in your way. It is the same spiritually. You need to put on the full armor of God so that you can take your stand against the devil's schemes.

Are you leaning on Him to guide you through life?

Channel Markers

You guide me with your counsel.
—Psalm 73:24

When you are traveling by boat, you may see many different navigational devices to give directions and warnings. They are different in color, with numbers, letters, and symbols written on them. To be seen at night, some have lights or gongs that ring by the movement of the water.

In the Intracoastal Waterway, there are channel markers showing boats the deep water. When a boat goes off course on either side of the markers, it can become stranded in the mud or sand, or be crushed on the rocks.

In channels where boats are docked, oblong buoys with the words "No wake" are telling boaters to go slow. The wake (the waves made by the passing boat) can cause the docked boats to rock and possibly cause damage.

Other markers or buoys explain why you cannot sail in a particular area. It shows the fishnet area or alerts you that a scuba diver is under the water or a regatta is taking place.

Not knowing the future, you can think of life like a boat sailing on unknown waters. The rules of the sea need to be followed. The rules and guidelines, or markers, that God gives you in the Bible must also be obeyed.

If you are not careful to follow God's Word, you can drift away from the Lord. You can be crushed by the world's influence. You may be trapped in a situation and not know how to overcome it.

The buoy saying "No wake" is the same as God asking you to slow down and wait for His answer as to the direction you should take. Waiting for God will never cause regrets.

The warning that you are near a fishnet area or a scuba diver is under the water could also be a warning that you are drifting complacently through life thinking there are no obstacles to your future plans, not realizing the devil is waiting to catch you in a moment of weakness or snare you in his net.

Even in the twilight of your life, it is important to start each day asking the Lord to show you His markers for the direction in which you should go.

Are you drifting through life, or are you listening to and heeding God's warnings?

Delays

Wait for the LORD; be strong and take
heart and wait for the LORD.
—Psalm 27:14

To celebrate their tenth anniversary, Margaret and Gary decided to go on a cruise. Their ship was scheduled to leave Saturday afternoon from Florida.

Margaret, on a business trip, flew from Atlantic City to Pittsburgh Friday night. She was to meet Gary there at the airport the next day. However, early Saturday morning found Gary pacing the Erie Airport as heavy fog delayed his flight. The Pittsburgh flight to Florida was due to depart soon.

Margaret anxiously looked for Gary. He still had not arrived by boarding time. When her row was called, she hesitantly boarded the plane. When told the plane would be leaving in five minutes, she worried, wondering if her husband would make this flight. Departure time came and went. A plumbing problem had been discovered.

Just before the repair was completed, Gary boarded the plane.

Many of the passengers, I'm sure, were unhappy with the delay. Margaret was glad for the delay. She could relax now that Gary was next to her.

God may be slow to respond according to your schedule, but He is never late for His divine purpose. "The Lord is not slow in keeping his promise, as some understand slowness. Instead he is patient with you, not wanting anyone to perish, but everyone to come to repentance" (2 Peter 3:9).

There is a reason for the delays in your life. God may be testing your faith in Him. It may be the wrong time for your request to be answered. By delaying His answer, God may be giving you the opportunity to give Him the glory, or someone else may be profiting from the delay.

Do you get impatient when events don't happen according to your schedule? Ask God to give you peace and patience while you wait, knowing He has a reason for everything that is happening in your life.

Remember, God is always on time.

American Express Card

But I will sing of your strength, in the morning
I will sing of your love; for you are my
fortress, my refuge in times of trouble.
—Psalm 59:16

The American Express credit card's slogan is "Don't leave home without it." You should make this your slogan with one important change: "Don't leave home without Jesus." Take Jesus Christ with you wherever you go.

Before you start rushing through the day, thank Him for being with you. Ask Him for help and guidance through all that needs to be done. Trust Him that He will answer your prayer.

"Let the morning bring me word of your unfailing love, for I have put my trust in you. Show me the way I should go, for to you I entrust my life" (Psalm 143:8).

Take Jesus with you to be your shield against temptation (1 Corinthians 10:13); to be your comforter in time of sorrow (2 Corinthians 1:3–4); to be your peace in the midst of trouble (Psalm 4:8); and to be your aide to pick you up when you fall

(Psalm 37:23–24). Do not go where Jesus would not go or you would not want Jesus to find you.

"Do not merely listen to the word, and so deceive yourselves. Do what it says. But whoever looks intently into the perfect law that gives freedom, and continues in it—not forgetting what they have heard, but doing it—they will be blessed in what they do" (James 1:22, 25).

Before leaving home, ask yourself, "Would Jesus want me to go there? Would I want Him finding me doing this? Would I want Him finding me where I am when He comes to call me home?"

Plaster Cast

Let us throw off everything that hinders and the
sin that so easily entangles. And let us run with
perseverance the race marked out for us.
—Hebrews 12:1

A plaster cast is made to keep an arm or leg from moving. Sin in your life, like a plaster cast, keeps you from having a close relationship with Jesus Christ.

When the cast is removed after an arm or leg has been immobilized for any length of time, the limb will be very weak. Only physical therapy and exercise will strengthen the arm or leg.

It is the same in your spiritual life. If you are harboring sin in your life or neglecting to read God's Word and not listening to what God is telling you, your spiritual life will regress and be weak.

"Surely the arm of the LORD is not too short to save, nor his ear too dull to hear. But your iniquities have separated you from your God; your sins have hidden his face from you, so that he will not hear" (Isaiah 59:1–2).

When you want to come back to God, you need to forget your pride, admit your sin, and ask Him to forgive you. God will forgive you.

"If my people, who are called by my name, will humble themselves and pray and seek my face and turn from their wicked ways, then I will hear from heaven, and will forgive their sin and will heal their land" (2 Chronicles 7:14).

Then spiritual therapy is needed. Ask God to help you understand His Word as you read it and follow through on what you read. This must be done every day to become stronger in your faith and to become more like Jesus Christ.

"Come near to God, and he will come near to you. Wash your hands, you sinners, and purify your hearts, you double-minded" (James 4:8).

Whoever seeks the Lord with his whole heart and keeps His laws is blessed with all spiritual blessings (Ephesians 1:3).

Are you letting sin keep you from having a close relationship with the Lord?

Clogged Vacuum Cleaner

Search me, God, and know my heart; test me and
know my anxious thoughts. See if there is any offensive
way in me, and lead me in the way everlasting.
—Psalm 139:23–24

While vacuuming the carpets, I noticed that the
vacuum cleaner stopped picking up the dirt.
I checked the bag. It was only half-full. The
belt was still good and in place. Then I looked at the nozzle.
A small safety pin was blocking the opening, preventing the
vacuum cleaner from working. After I removed the pin, the
vacuum cleaner again picked up the dirt.

Your spiritual life can be the same. Allowing any type of
sin can block the Holy Spirit working in your life and close off
your relationship with Jesus Christ.

"Surely the arm of the LORD is not too short to save, nor
his ear too dull to hear. But your iniquities have separated you
from your God; your sins have hidden his face from you, so
that he will not hear" (Isaiah 59:1).

You are told to "Get rid of all bitterness, rage and anger,
brawling and slander, along with every form of malice. Be kind

and compassionate to one another, forgiving each other just as in Christ God forgave you" (Ephesians 4:31–32).

Are you asking God to show you if anything in your life is blocking your relationship with Him?

Jammed Fax Machine

All scripture is God-breathed and is useful for
teaching, rebuking, correcting- and training in
righteousness, so that the servant of God may be
thoroughly equipped for every good work.
—2 Timothy 3:16

The paper was jammed in the fax machine. The easiest
way to release the paper appeared to be to cut it and
pull it out with tweezers.

The last few inches refused to come out. After twenty-
eight frustrating minutes, I referred to the instruction manual.
All that needed to be done was to squeeze two levers, lift the
top, and take out the paper.

If I had read the manual in the beginning, I would have
saved myself a lot of time and aggravation, and possibly a
ruined machine.

You have the Bible. It is God's Word, His instruction book,
your manual for living a life that pleases the Lord. Principles
and behavior patterns are given in Colossians, chapter 3,
that will guide you in every situation in which you may find
yourselves. "Be diligent in these matters; give yourself wholly

to them, so that everyone may see your progress. Watch your life and doctrine closely" (1 Timothy 4:15–16).

Prayer and meditating on God's Word is a daily necessity. All believers need to follow through on what they read to avoid having regrets over wasted time and lost opportunities to be witnesses for Christ.

Are you meditating daily on God's Word for guidance? Are you following through on what you read?

Demolition

Be alert and of sober mind. Your enemy the devil prowls
around like a roaring lion looking for someone to devour.
—1 Peter 5:8

I watched an older home being demolished in one day. The
backhoe kept tearing at the house until it was only rubble.
I wondered how long it took to build that house and how
many years people called it home.

If you are not careful, your life can be the same as that
older home. Many years of being a faithful servant of Christ
can be torn down little by little. This erosion often begins by
allowing little temptations to overtake you. Your reputation
of being a Christian can also be torn down by one action or
reaction, or by one wrong decision or indecision.

It is necessary to put on the whole armor of God to
withstand everything that the devil puts in your way to ruin
your testimony for Christ. "Put on the full armor of God, so
that you can take your stand against the devil's schemes. For
our struggle is not against flesh and blood, but against the
rulers, against the authorities, against the powers of this dark

world and against the spiritual forces of evil in the heavenly realms" (Ephesians 6:11–12).

You need to gird your waist with truth and put on the breastplate of righteousness, which you have in Christ. Also, put on your feet sandals with the gospel of peace and cling to the shield of faith to stop the devil's darts of doubting God. Take the helmet of salvation and the sword of the Spirit, which is the word of God, and always pray for help, wisdom, and discernment.

Your adversary, the devil, is just like the backhoe. He does not give up in his quest to ruin your efforts to draw near to the Lord and live for Him. The devil knows your Achilles' heel and will try to use it.

God has promised to give you a way out of any temptation the devil puts in your way. "No temptation has overtaken you except what is common to mankind. And God is faithful; he will not let you be tempted beyond what you can bear. But when you are tempted, he will also provide a way out so that you endure it" (1 Corinthians 10:13).

Are you submitting yourself to God and resisting the devil?

Prayer Partners

When Moses' hands grew tired, they took a stone and
put it under him and he sat on it. Aaron and Hur held
his hands up—one on one side, one on the other—so
that his hands remained steady till sunset. So Joshua
overcame the Amalekite army with the sword.
—Exodus 17:12–13

I realized my husband's hearing aids were missing after
everything was unpacked and put away. I was sure I had
packed Bill's hearing aids in the tan plastic grocery bag
with many other small items before leaving our daughter's
home. I phoned my daughter, asking her to look for them. She
heard the stress in my voice and sensed that I was very upset.
She said she would look, even though she was sure I had taken
them. She would also pray, asking the Lord to calm me and
open my eyes to find them.

Later that afternoon, the Lord pressed on my mind to take
the bag out of the trash and look again. As I lifted the bag out
of the trash, the hearing aids fell out.

Just as Moses needed Aaron and Hur to help him, you may need a prayer partner to pray with you and for you. Or someone may need you for a prayer partner.

You are told to pray without stopping (1 Thessalonians 5:17). There are times when you need to persevere in your prayers. Remember, Daniel had to pray for twenty-one days for an answer because the devil was interfering (Daniel 10:15).

When you do not know what to pray, the Holy Spirit will help you. "In the same way, the Spirit helps us in our weakness. We do not know what we ought to pray for, but the Spirit himself intercedes for us through wordless groans" (Romans 8:26).

Are you a prayer partner when someone asks you for help to overcome a problem or make an important decision?

Missed Opportunity

Therefore, as we have opportunity, let us do
good to all people, especially to those who
belong to the family of believers.
—Galatians 6:10

The sign said a certain motel was down the road. After driving a few miles, I decided the sign was wrong. I turned around and took a different motel of a lower caliber that I had passed. Getting gas the next morning, I asked about the other motel and was told it was a mile further down the road.

By not going a little farther, and by thinking I knew more than the authorities who put up the hotel sign, I missed sleeping in a better motel with a sink that worked, a computer line, and a better continental breakfast.

If you are not careful, your Christian life can be the same. If you only follow Christ halfway, without doing whatever the Lord lays on your heart to do or taking the opportunity to show other people God's love for them, you lose the blessing He wants to give you.

When asking the Lord for anything, have patience and a listening ear to be sure that what you decide is what the Lord wants you to do and what He wants for you. An eagle sometimes pushes the eaglet out of the nest so it will learn to fly. God may push you to get out of your complacency and your comfort zone so your faith in Him will grow.

"'For I know the plans I have for you,' declares the Lord, 'plans to prosper you and not to harm you, plans to give you hope and a future'" (Jeremiah 29:1). When God lays it on your heart to do something for Him, do you think up excuses or only go halfway?

Are you listening to the Lord so you can grow in faith and looking for the opportunities to show His love to the people with whom you come into contact?

Don't miss His blessings by thinking you know what is best.

Pelicans

But those who hope in the LORD will renew their strength.
They will soar on wings like eagles; they will run and
not grow weary, they will walk and not be faint.
—Isaiah 40:31

One windy day, I watched the pelicans flying over the ocean. Their wings were spread wide and held still while floating on the wind's currents. God brought the above verse to my mind.

You can have peace by spreading your wings of faith wide, trusting God to show you how to overcome or work through your problems. When taking your problems to God, you need to have faith that He will answer. God's answer can be to remove the problem or to help you to work through the problem.

When you doubt, God will not answer (James 1:5–8). Faith is the key to answered prayer. When your faith wavers, go to the Lord and tell Him how you are feeling and what you are thinking. Ask Him to help you to restore your faith in Him. He will.

When you trust and lean on God, He gives you peace that is unexplainable. "Do not be anxious about anything, but in every situation, by prayer and petition, with thanksgiving, present your requests to God. And the peace of God, which transcends all understanding, will guard your hearts and minds in Christ Jesus" (Philippians 4:6, 7).

Many times, when you trust other people, they fail to follow through on their word. "It is better take refuge in the LORD than to trust in humans" (Psalm 118:8).

God keeps all His promises. "Let us hold unswervingly to the hope we profess, for he who promised is faithful" (Hebrews 10:23).

God wants to help us, and He tells us to come boldly to Him for help when we need it (Hebrews 4:16).

Are you taking your problems to God, trusting Him to help you during your trials?

Rules

Whoever believes in him is not condemned, but whoever
does not believe stands condemned already because they
have not believed in the name of God's one and only Son.
—John 3:18

Rules and penalties must be adhered to, from the
easiest to the most complicated game or race. When
a participant does not follow the rules, he or she is
disqualified and often kept out of the game.

Life is not a game! But there are rules that God has
established and that must be obeyed. They are found in the
Bible.

No one can add to or subtract from God's commands.
Not one word can be added or substituted for a person's
convenience.

"Do not add to what I command you, and do not subtract
from it, but keep the commands of the LORD your God that
I give you" (Deuteronomy 4:2). God gave Moses the Ten
Commandments (Exodus 20:1–17) as the standard to follow.

The first commandment was not to have any other gods
before the Lord. Jesus took it a step further and said, "Love

the Lord your God with all your heart and with all your soul and with all your mind. This is the first and greatest commandment. And the second is like it: 'Love your neighbor as yourself.' All the Law and the Prophets hang on these two commandments" (Matthew 22:37–40).

A person has to follow all ten commandments. Not one can be broken. No one can keep all ten commandments. Therefore, God, in His mercy, provided a way for everyone to have a close relationship with Christ and to spend eternity with Him in heaven.

It is by accepting Christ as Savior and believing that His death on the cross is the only way the penalty for sin can be—and is—paid. It is a free gift from God (Ephesians 2:8–9).

Are you making your own rules or living by God's rules?

Sailing

"For my thoughts are not your thoughts, neither
are your ways my ways," declares the Lord.
—Isaiah 55:8

Since sailing looked easy, my husband and I decided to rent a sailboat. Casting off and sailing into the bay was not a problem. Our trouble started when we tried to tack into the wind to go home.

The first time, we turned to the starboard side, only to go away from the shore. The next time we tried to tack into the wind, we reversed the process. We were wrong again. With each attempt, we kept sailing farther and farther into the bay.

Realizing our predicament, I prayed, "Lord, please help us work the sail and rudder correctly." I wanted to show the rest of the family that we could sail, without a problem, on our first attempt.

Knowing we were in trouble, we called to three boys who were riding by in a small boat with an outboard motor. We asked if they could tow us to shore. We were told to tie their tossed rope to the cleat on the bow of our boat and to take the sail down. We were glad to do it, knowing we were being taken safely home.

Taking the sail down is the same as getting rid of any prideful feeling that you do not need the Lord. Tying the boys' rope to the cleat on the boat symbolizes trusting the Lord to help you through every circumstance in life.

The Lord answered my prayer—not the way I asked, but His way. He knew my prideful heart and had to show me that pride does not belong in a Christian's life.

"For everything in the world—the lust of the flesh, the lust of the eyes, and the pride of life—comes not from the Father but from the world" (1 John 2:16).

Are you letting your pride interfere with the way the Lord knows how to help?

Postponed Vacation

Many are the plans in a person's heart, but
it is the LORD's purpose that prevails.
—Proverbs 19:21

Mae and I had our summer planned, with a tour of
several midwestern states in June. But God said,
"No! Not at this time."

By God postponing our trip, we were blessed in four
different ways.

Mae had a small stroke, rendering her left hand useless.
The following week, I slipped and fell, hitting my back on a
doorjamb.

Mae's stroke was a blessing. During her many tests, the
doctors found a problem with her heart. Since the problem
has been corrected, she feels better physically than she has for
many years. With physical therapy, Mae is now able to use
her hand.

Another blessing that came with being home: Mae was
there to check out the loud banging noise in her attic. The attic
fan was hanging by two bolts instead of four. If the fan had

broken completely loose, live wires hitting each other could have caused sparks and started a fire while she was away.

For two weeks, the bed and a recliner were my constant companions. During that time, God took me off my high horse. He made me realize that my good health and the ability to come and go were blessings from Him. They were not things to take for granted or to make me think that I can do all these things without God's help.

"Pride goes before destruction, a haughty spirit before a fall" (Proverbs 16:18).

Another blessing was that June was a very hot month in the midwestern states from all the forest fires. The smoke from the fires clouded the views of many interesting sights and attractions. In September, the weather was cool and the atmosphere was clear, perfect for traveling and sightseeing.

When you ask God for guidance as to when and where to go on vacation, God will interfere when He knows there is a better time or a better place.

Do you fight the postponements God puts in your way?

Troubles

When you pass through the waters, I will be with you;
and when you pass through the rivers, they shall not
sweep over you. When you walk through the fire, you
will not be burned; the flames will not set you ablaze.
—Isaiah 43:2

During my routine dental checkup, I jokingly told the dentist, "I won't like you if you tell me I have some cavities."

After telling the dentist what I was thinking, I had a thought. When a crisis comes in your life—circumstances that cannot be controlled or that you do not like—you have the option to blame God and stop having fellowship with Him through not praying nor reading the Bible.

Or you can take the best option: to be steadfast in your faith and lean on God, knowing only He can give you the comfort you need. Also remembering that He promised never to leave nor forsake you and that He will uphold you with His righteous right hand.

Having leaned on God for comfort through your trials, and remembering how He has comforted you, you are then able to encourage and comfort other people who are going through the same circumstances.

"Praise be to the God and Father of our Lord Jesus Christ, the Father of compassion and the God of all comfort, who comforts us in all our troubles, so that we can comfort those in any trouble with the comfort we ourselves receive from God" (2 Corinthians 1:3, 4).

When you do not understand why life is not going the way you like it, remember that God is in control. He may be testing you or using it for His glory. Or He may want to give you something better.

"Consider it pure joy, my brothers and sisters, whenever you face trials of many kinds, because you know that the testing of your faith produces perseverance. Let perseverance finish its work so that you may be mature and complete, not lacking anything" (James 1:2–4).

In your troubles, do you blame God and push Him out of your life, or do you look to Him for comfort?

Seagulls

Keep reminding God's people of these things. Warn
them before God against quarreling about words; it
is of no value, and only ruins those who listen.
—2 Timothy 2:14

Every morning, I throw out bread for the herring gulls
who are waiting on the neighbor's roof. One morning,
two herring gulls were arguing and continued to argue
even after I threw out the bread. A laughing gull flew in and
ate it all.

This caused me to think of the people who continually
speak of their dislike of the church's format, the sermons
chosen, or the presentation of the sermon.

Listen to the words of Titus 3:9. "But avoid foolish
controversies and genealogies and arguments about the law,
because these are unprofitable and useless."

This may be the only time that a particular topic will be
discussed. When we come to church, our cares and prejudices
need to be left outside. To get the full benefit of the sermon,
our minds should be concentrating on what is being taught.

It also reminded me of people who seem to find a complaint in their vocation, relationships, even the weather.

In any conversation, be careful of the topics you discuss. Also, you should not gossip or stretch the truth to make a story more interesting. It is better to keep your thoughts to yourself if they will cause an argument about anything that does not matter.

"Avoid godless chatter, because those who indulge in it will become more and more ungodly" (2 Timothy 2:16).

"Therefore, rid yourselves of all malice and all deceit, hypocrisy, envy, and slander of every kind" (1 Peter 2:1).

Before getting into a worthless conversation, ask yourself, "Will this bring honor to the Lord?"

Are you wasting your time discussing subjects that do not matter? Are your conversations helpful and encouraging?

The Missed Package

The LORD is near to all who call on him, to all who
call on him in truth. He fulfills the desires of those
who fear him; he hears their cry and saves them.
—Psalm 145:18–19

The men who were working for my husband needed a
special part that was being shipped COD. It was for
a factory's electrical panel. Receiving that part was
crucial. The job needed to be completed that day.

I waited impatiently at the office for United Parcel Service
(UPS) to deliver the package until it was time to leave for a
doctor's appointment. Before I left, I asked the Lord, "Please
don't let United Parcel Service come until I return because that
part is needed today."

However, my appointment took longer than expected.
When I came back to the office, I found the note saying
UPS had been there and that the package would be delivered
tomorrow.

Before I left the office to look for the truck, I asked the
Lord to help me. I did not want to be the cause for missing
this important delivery.

Slowly driving down the town's main street, I stopped at each intersection. I looked left and right for the UPS truck. After driving slowly for five blocks, I saw the driver sitting on the curb reading a book while waiting for the mechanic to come and change a flat tire.

Proverbs 3:5–6 says, "Trust in the LORD with all your heart and lean not on your own understanding; in all your ways submit to him, and he will make your paths straight."

Before leaving for the doctor, it was time to pray and wait. Returning to the office, finding the note, it was time to pray for guidance in locating the truck. Chapter three of Ecclesiastes tells us that there are times to pray and wait and there are times to pray and take action.

When asking the Lord for guidance, do you ask if you should wait or if you should act?

Wrong Exit

You, Lord, are forgiving and good, abounding
in love to all who call to you.
—Psalm 86:5

Have you ever traveled on a superhighway, driving at a fast pace, and realized you had missed your exit because you were in the wrong lane or were distracted? Then the only way is to go many miles out of your way to return to the correct exit.

Your Christian life, if you are not careful, can be the same. Rushing busily through the day, distracted by all the things you want to accomplish, playing on the computer, or watching the programs on television, you neglect to take time to read the Bible and talk to the Lord.

Time has a way of slipping through your fingers faster than you realize, just like traveling many miles past the correct exit. The time you spend out of fellowship with the Lord cannot be reclaimed.

To get back to where you were in your spiritual life, you need to come back to the Lord with your whole heart, confessing your sin and asking for His forgiveness. "'You will seek me and find me when you seek me with all your heart. I will be found by you,' declares the LORD, 'and will bring you back from captivity'"(Jeremiah 29:13–14).

When you are again in fellowship with the Lord, be sure to spend time praying, studying the Bible, and memorizing Bible verses. It is necessary to take the time to listen to what the Lord is telling you. Then follow through on what you are told.

Are you taking time to ask for guidance and heeding what the Lord is saying?

Balls

If you love me, keep my commands. And I will ask the
Father, and he will give you another advocate to help
you and be with you forever—the Spirit of truth.
—John 14:15–17

F ootball, tennis, volleyball, and soccer are all different
sports. Yet, they have one common denominator: a ball.
Each ball is a different size or shape, but they are all
filled with air. A ball only half-filled with air cannot be used
effectively, and a flat ball cannot be used at all.

Christians are found in every race and color. They have
different occupations, vocations, and talents, but they all have
one common denominator: the Holy Spirit. When you accept
Christ as your Savior, you are given the Holy Spirit for help
and guidance.

Just as balls need to be filled with air, Christians need to
let the Holy Spirit in every area of their lives. People who do
not let the Holy Spirit in every area of their lives are not letting
God use them to their full potential. He will not force His way
into your life.

"Do not get drunk on wine, which leads to debauchery. Instead, be filled with the Spirit" (Ephesians 5:18).

The Holy Spirit is a person, and you are told not to quench Him by not listening to Him. You are not to grieve the Holy Spirit by living a life that is not honoring to God.

The Holy Spirit will only work in your life as you let Him. "Now to him who is able to do immeasurably more than all we ask or imagine, according to his power that is at work within us" (Ephesians 3:20).

Are you letting the Holy Spirit rule in every area of your life?

Vehicles

Since, then, you have been raised with Christ,
set your hearts on things above, where Christ
is, seated at the right hand of God.
—Colossians 3:1

Motor vehicles come in all shapes, sizes, and colors. They are made for racing, hauling, pleasure, and transportation. License plates are required to show who is the owner and his or her home state.

God created people with different colors, temperaments, and feelings. Hobbies, occupations, and vocations vary.

Some people are like racing cars, racing through each day from one pleasure to seek another. They are seldom content.

Other people are like trucks, filling their lives with the accumulation of wealth or articles. God says you are not to hoard material items that can disappear. You are to build your treasure in heaven, where it is safe (Matthew 6:19–21).

Christians should be like transporting vehicles, living their lives being helpers and encouragers. They should not be consumed with what can be collected, but what can be given back to God.

We are told to "Command them to do good, to be rich in good deeds, and to be generous and willing to share" (1 Timothy 6:18).

As a license plate shows the home state of the vehicle and the owner, our lifestyle should reflect the Holy Spirit living within us. "Keep your lives free from the love of money and be content with what you have, because God said, 'Never will I leave you; never will I forsake you'" (Hebrews 13:5).

As a Christian, does your lifestyle, the way you look, your conversations, and actions show that you are only traveling through this world and that your eternal home is in heaven?

Forgotten Tool

For your Father knows what you need before you ask Him.
—Matthew 6:8

Kathy called her father, telling him her hot water heater had sprung a leak. She asked him if he knew where to buy a new hot water heater and the name of a plumber in her area. Her father replied, "I'll bring it with me and install it myself."

As Kathy called her father, God wants us to call on Him and trust Him to help. "Let us then approach God's throne of grace with confidence, so that we may receive mercy and find grace to help us in our time of need" (Hebrews 4:16).

While installing the hot water heater, her father realized he had forgotten to bring one necessary tool. God, knowing Bill would need the tool he had forgotten, had the builder's appointment to put in a new window insert be at the same time that Bill would be there. Kathy asked the builder if he had the necessary tool. He let her father use it.

God knows your needs even before you do. "Before they call, I will answer; while they are still speaking, I will hear" (Isaiah 65:24).

"But when you ask, you must believe and not doubt, because the one who doubts is like a wave of the sea, blown and tossed by the wind. That person should not expect anything from the Lord. Such a person is double-minded and unstable in all they do"(James 1:6–8).

After receiving your answer, thank God for hearing, listening and answering. "Give thanks in all circumstances; for this is God's will for you in Christ Jesus" (1 Thessalonians 5:18).

When God has answered your prayer and helped you, do you thank Him?

Car Maintenance

Do your best to present yourself to God as one
approved, a worker who does not need to be ashamed
and who correctly handles the word of truth.
—2 Timothy 2:15

To keep a car running in top form, it is necessary to give
it the proper care and maintenance. As you maintain
your car, you need to maintain your spiritual life.

After a certain number of miles, the oil needs to be
changed. Your thoughts need to be changed from thinking
as the world thinks. Your thoughts need to be focused on
Christ, just as your car lights need to be focused in the right
direction. Studying God's Word and prayer to keep you
growing spiritually are the same as the transmission, brakes,
and power steering needing the proper amount and the correct
oil to keep these parts lubricated and moving.

Having the tires on your car filled with air so you don't feel
all the bumps in the road is the same as letting the Holy Spirit
into every area of your life to guide you to avoid temptations
and help you through the rough parts in your life.

Seat belts need to be worn and kept tight to help avoid injuries in an accident. You need to keep close to Christ to avoid slipping into the old worldly habits and losing your close relationship with Christ.

If the battery is not charged, nothing works. The same is true in your spiritual life. Without Christ, your life has no lasting meaning and no hope of spending eternity with Him. Christ told us, "Without me, you can do nothing."

You need to ask yourself, "Am I letting the Holy Spirit in every area of my life? Are my thoughts focused on what God is telling me? Am I walking close to God?"

Are you keeping a close watch on every aspect of your spiritual life?

Candid Camera

I eagerly expect and hope that I will in no way be ashamed,
but will have sufficient courage so that now as always Christ
will be exalted in my body, whether by life or by death.
—Philippians 1:20

"Smile, you're on *Candid Camera!*" was a phrase heard on a popular television show in the 1950s and 1960s. It was entertaining to see people's responses in action or words in awkward or tempting circumstances. When they realized they had been watched and recorded, no doubt some of the people on *Candid Camera* wished they could recall what they had said or that they had reacted differently.

More important than being on *Candid Camera* is knowing God is watching and recording. He knows our intentions in what we are doing. "The eyes of the LORD are everywhere, keeping watch on the wicked and the good" (Proverbs 15:3).

I was at a funeral sitting next to the aisle when three people started talking about a relative of the deceased. It was a lesson to be careful in all your conversations, for you never know who is listening.

You also need to be careful of your actions and reactions. They speak louder than words. You should practice what you preach. People do not always remember the circumstances, but they do remember what has been said or done. As a spring cannot produce fresh and salt water at the same time, a Christian's conversation should always be free of gossip and demeaning someone.

"With the tongue we praise our Lord and Father, and with it we curse human beings, who have been made in God's likeness. Out of the same mouth come praise and cursing. My brothers and sisters, this should not be" (James 3:9–10).

Before speaking you should ask the Lord, "Set a guard over my mouth, LORD; keep watch over the door of my lips" (Psalm 141:3).

Are your actions and reactions showing Christ is the Lord and master of your life?

To Buy or to Build

Then Gideon said to God, "Do not be angry with me. Let
me make just one more request. Allow me one more test
with the fleece, but this time make the fleece dry and let the
ground be covered with dew." That night God did so. Only
the fleece was dry; all the ground was covered with dew.
—Judges 6:39–40

My husband and I wanted to buy a house at the
shore in New Jersey. My only request: it had to
be on a waterfront lot.

We looked at houses and lots. There was a lot for sale on a
cove. Mr. Adams, the owner and a builder, discussed the pros
and cons of building a new house and renovating an older
house.

We decided to build a new house. Mr. Adams said he
would have all the legal documents drawn up by the following
weekend.

That night, Bill had second thoughts. He was not sure
about building a new house. He did know about renovating
and could visualize a house completed. It would be the fifth
house we would renovate.

Bill called Mr. Adams and told him we had decided not to buy the lot. A single-family home was bought on a canal. After working six months to have the house the way we wanted, Bill was tired of spending weekends working and didn't feel like putting any more money or labor into it.

We saw another house that was different. An artist owned it. I prayed, "Father, if we are meant to have this house, please have the real estate agent call us before we leave the shore on Sunday." The call never came.

Another weekend was spent looking at houses. We saw a house we liked. It was being sold by a different real estate agency, and we agreed to the selling price.

On the way home, I realized I had not asked God about buying the house. I prayed, "Father, we signed the agreement of sale to buy this house without asking you. If we are to have it, okay. If we are not to have it, please throw a monkey wrench into the deal."

The following weekend, we were told the owners had decided not to sell. The agency offered to drop the percentage of their commission. The owners still would not sell. We were back to square one. We decided to call Mr. Adams. He gladly came with all the legal documents he had drawn up over six months ago.

Many neighbors have come and gone in the fifty years we have lived here. We have never regretted buying the lot and having the new house built.

Do you ask God to show you what your decision should be? Will you accept His answer?

Closed Doors

When they came to the border to Mysia, they tried to enter
Bithynia, but the Spirit of Jesus would not allow them to.
—Acts 16:7

Having lived in Japan for three years, Lois was determined to go on an elephant safari in Chiang Mai, Thailand, before returning to the United States. She arrived at the airport with her sick husband, Chris, and three excited, impatient children.

At the ticket counter, they were told the airplane was undergoing routine maintenance. They could take a flight on another airline that was ready to leave in fifteen minutes.

Arriving out of breath, they watched the gate being closed. Walking back to the original ticket counter, Lois angrily told God, "You could have made it possible to catch that flight. Why didn't you?"

Determined and stubborn, Lois accepted the next available flight, in eleven hours. It would arrive in Bangkok at one o'clock in the morning, with a connecting flight to Chiang Mai at six o'clock.

The airline would arrange a room at a hotel where they could sleep. Halfway through the flight, her family asleep on the plane, Lois was telling God that He could have prevented all of this. Then the stewardess came and told her, "We are sorry, but all the rooms in Bangkok are booked due to three big conventions. No rooms are available."

Lois replied, "Then we will sleep on the airport floor." Again, Lois asked God, "Why didn't you have one room open?"

At five o'clock, Lois and her family went to catch their connecting flight. The attendant at the counter told Lois, "There is a small problem. Only four seats, not five, were available."

Again God closed the door. It was the third time. To this, Chris said, "We are staying in Bangkok!"

Lois angrily told God again, "You could have prevented this. Why didn't you?"

God graciously arranged for one hotel to have a reservation cancelled. The first week, Chris was too sick to join Lois and the children in seeing different sights.

Reclining by the pool the second week, Chris read a story in the Sunday paper about an elephant safari in Chiang Mai. The lead elephant had gone mad, thrown the guide and a guest off its back, and trampled them to death. Another frightened elephant had thrown two people off its back, and one of them was in critical condition. It was the safari Lois had chosen.

Lois thanked the Lord that He had closed the doors, despite her persistence and questioning, and asked to be forgiven. Her oldest son had said many times that he wanted to ride on the lead elephant. Life would never have been the same if God had opened the doors for them to go on that safari.

God closes doors for your good because He can see the entire situation from the beginning to the end.

Do you keep trying to push open the doors you want opened, or do you have the faith to accept the closed doors God puts in your way?

Medication

And if the Spirit of him who raised Jesus from
the dead is living in you, he who raised Christ
from the dead will also give life to your mortal
bodies because of his Spirit who lives in you.
—Romans 8:11

Anyone using a medication to raise hemoglobin in the blood to the correct level needs iron for the medication to be completely beneficial.

As the medication needs iron to build up the necessary hemoglobin level, Christians needs the Holy Spirit, who lives within them, to help them live their lives in the way that glorifies God.

"Do you not know that your bodies are temples of the Holy Spirit, who is in you, whom you have received from God? You are not your own; you were bought at a price. Therefore, honor God with your bodies" (1 Corinthians 6:19–20).

The Holy Spirit is given to guide you and help in every circumstance, but He can only guide and help you as you let Him. The more you let the Holy Spirit into every area your life, the more He will be able to use you beyond your understanding.

"Now to Him who is able to do immeasurably more than all we ask or imagine, according to his power that is at work within us" (Ephesians 3:20).

He also guarantees your eternal inheritance with Jesus Christ in heaven. "Now it is God who makes both us and you stand firm in Christ. He anointed us, set his seal of ownership on us, and put his Spirit in our hearts as a deposit, guaranteeing what is to come" (2 Corinthians 1:21, 22).

Are you letting the Holy Spirit work in every area of your life?

Choices

Choose for yourselves this day whom you will serve.
—Joshua 24:15

Have you counted the many choices you make in a day? Every choice a person makes for a minor or major decision will often affect not only that person but many times other people. The consequences may be felt at once or not until many years later.

The main and most important choice all people have to make is whom they will follow and serve. That decision will determine how they will live their lives and where they will spend eternity.

No one can sit on a fence with one leg in the devil's territory and one leg in the presence of Jesus Christ, for "No one can serve two masters. Either you will hate the one and love the other, or you will be devoted to the one and despise the other. You cannot serve both God and money" (Matthew 6:24).

This is the life servants of Christ should live. They are not to lie or be bitter; they are not to sin when they are angry; they are not to steal but work so they can give to those who have need; they are not to grieve the Holy Spirit, but need to be careful what they say; they are to be kind to one another and forgive one another as God in Christ forgave them (Ephesians 4:24–32).

You are to be content with whatever you have, for God promised to supply all your needs (Philippians 4:19).

Jesus says in John 12:26, "Whoever serves me must follow me; and where I am, my servant also will be. My father will honor the one that serves me."

Serving the devil is easy because it is a life of doing what a person wants to do. His reward is having that person spending eternity with him in the lake of fire (Revelation 20:15).

Living a life serving Jesus Christ is not always easy, but He has promised to be with and help whoever follows Him (Isaiah 41:13). His followers also have the assurance that they will be spending eternity with Him in heaven (Philippians 3:20).

Will your choice be the same as Joshua's? "But for me and my house, we will serve the LORD" (Joshua 24:15).

Whom have you chosen to serve?

Two Black Dogs

For He will command his angels concerning
you to guard you in all your ways.
—Psalm 91:11

While vacationing in Florida, my husband, Bill, and I, with our daughter and our three granddaughters, decided to visit Pine Island, where the movie *PT 109* had been filmed.

The ride to the island in our small boat was smooth and relaxing. We moored the boat to the remains of a dock and walked around the southern end of the island. A large, sandy beach and some trees were the only things to be seen. We did not see any birds or animals.

Bill felt adventurous and decided to return home by going around the other side of the island. It was a bad decision.

Riding was going smoothly halfway around the other side when the motor stopped running properly. We were caught in lots of loose coral. Everyone had to get out of the boat. Walking through the coral was the same as walking in thick mud, and we often sank in up to our knees. We continued to plod and push the boat through the thickening coral.

The girls complained; my daughter and I told Bill what we thought of his idea. The only person who did not say a word was Bill.

Instead of complaining, I should have been asking the Lord for strength to keep our legs moving and to show us the best route to take.

As we turned the northeast corner of the island, heading toward home and hopefully into deep water, two large, barking dogs came from the next small island. I thought, *Oh no!* Were we in a place where we should not be?

Instead of swimming directly to us, they swam ahead of us. They continued to bark as they showed us the way where the coral was easy to walk through and to a very narrow opening of cloudy water leading back to the open bay.

When we were able to climb back into the boat, the dogs left us. We were glad to be able to drop the motor back into the water and let it push us home.

I didn't ask, but the Lord knew we needed help. I thanked the Lord for always keeping His promise to never leave us nor forsake us, for watching over us and sending those two black, barking dogs to guide us (Deuteronomy 31:8).

The Lord uses many ways to help you in time of trouble.

Do you recognize the Lord's answer to your prayer?

Foundation

For no one can lay any foundation other than
the one already laid, which is Jesus Christ.
—1 Corinthians 3:11

Watching the foundation being laid, I wondered what type of building would be built.

As a child of God, you are told to be careful how you build on the foundation that is Christ.

"If anyone builds on this foundation using gold, silver, costly stones, wood, hay, or straw, their work will be shown for what it is, because the Day will bring it to light. It will be revealed with fire, and the fire will test the quality of each person's work. If what has been built survives, the builder will receive a reward" (1 Corinthians 3:12–14).

Are you building on this foundation on a daily basis or occasionally? Gold, silver, and precious stones are the deeds you are doing so that God may be glorified. The wood, hay, and straw are the deeds you are building for self-recognition and pride.

God warns you in Matthew 6:1–4 not to brag about what you do. If you talk about it to get the praise of men, then you have your reward.

Even small actions done with love for Christ will be rewarded. God loves a cheerful giver (2 Corinthians 9:7). It is not what you do or give, but the way each act is done and your attitude when you do it. It may be a small action on your part and yet mean very much to the recipient.

The Lord promised that He is coming again and will bring your reward with Him.

"Look, I am coming soon! My reward is with me, and I will give to each person according to what they have done" (Revelation 22:12).

Is your spiritual foundation the Lord Jesus Christ? What are you building on it? How often are you adding to it?

The Laughing Gull

Let us then approach God's throne of grace with
confidence, so that we may receive mercy and
find grace to help us in our time of need.
—Hebrews 4:16

I learned a lesson in perseverance from a laughing gull. Early in the morning, only one laughing gull comes boldly and waits patiently on the top step by the kitchen door for me to feed him. After he is fed, he flies away.

When he comes back in the afternoon, sometimes I will throw crackers to him as soon as I see him, and at other times, I have him wait for a hand-out. He will wait and wait, never taking his eyes from the kitchen door.

Just like that laughing gull who sits and waits patiently, Christians must come daily and boldly before the throne of God's grace for help and wait patiently until God answers.

The laughing gull knows I will feed him. We, also, have the assurance that God will answer our prayers if we persevere and do not waver.

"So I say unto you: Ask and it will be given to you; seek and you will find; knock and the door will be opened to you.

For everyone who asks receives; the one who seeks finds; and to the one who knocks the door will be opened" (Luke 11:9–10).

Sometimes this gull will call the other birds sitting on the neighbor's roof to share the food with him. Another lesson learned. We should share the blessings God gives us when we are able.

The laughing gull knows that when I close the kitchen door, there will be no more food. God never closes the door.

"The eyes of the LORD are on the righteous, and his ears are attentive to their cry" (Psalm 34:15).

Are you coming to God for help and waiting patiently for His answer?

The Judge

Let all creation rejoice before the LORD, for he comes,
he comes to judge the earth. He will judge the world
in righteousness and the peoples in his faithfulness.
—Psalm 96:13

After an automobile accident, I had to stand alone before a judge. Looking up at him sitting high above me, not knowing what to expect, I wondered if he was just and compassionate or a harsh sentencing judge.

Standing there before him, I thought that someday everyone will stand before a greater and a much more important judge. A judge who is just and knows all your thoughts and the motives behind your actions.

The Lord is coming again to judge everyone's work. No one knows the exact time. God will be sitting on a great white throne and will open books to judge everyone's works according to their knowledge of Him and their reaction to that knowledge (Revelation 20:11–12).

You alone are responsible for your past actions and reactions. You cannot blame anyone for the way you acted.

"Do not be deceived: God cannot be mocked. A man reaps what he sows. Whoever sows to please their flesh, from the flesh will reap destruction; whoever sows to please the Spirit, from the Spirit will reap eternal life" (Galatians 6:7–8).

Many will be surprised that they will not spend eternity with God and Christ. "Not everyone who says to me, 'Lord, Lord,' will enter the kingdom of heaven, but only the one who does the will of my Father who is in heaven. Many will say to me on that day, 'Lord, Lord, did we not prophesy in your name and in your name drive out demons and in your name perform many miracles?' Then I will tell them plainly, 'I never knew you. Away from me, you evildoers!'" (Matthew 7:21–23).

Are you ready to stand before God?

The Advocate

For there is one God and one mediator between
God and mankind, the man Christ Jesus, who
gave himself as a ransom for all people.
—1 Timothy 2:5–6

While waiting my turn to stand before the judge, I noticed several people had lawyers pleading their cases, hoping the judge would be lenient. My thoughts turned to the above verse.

Unlike the lawyers hoping to win their cases, Jesus Christ, our advocate and High Priest, paid the price to cover all our past, present, and future sins. He is now seated on the right hand of God interceding for us.

"But if anyone does sin, we have an advocate with the Father—Jesus Christ, the Righteous One" (1 John 2:1).

As the High Priest, Jesus Christ, is able to forgive you your sins, if you ask Him (1 John 1:9).

Jesus Christ as the High Priest (Hebrews 4:14) can sympathize with all your weaknesses. While living on earth, He felt all the emotions you may have felt: hunger (Matthew 4:2), tiredness (John 4:6), sadness (John 11:35), and temptation, yet without sin (Hebrews 4:15).

Today, Jesus is knocking on your heart's door asking to be your Savior and advocate. He will not force His way; you need to open the door and let Him in.

"Here I am! I stand at the door and knock. If anyone hears my voice and opens the door, I will come in and eat with that person, and they with me" (Revelation 3:20).

Will you open your heart's door and accept Jesus Christ to be your Savior and advocate to intercede for you and as your High Priest to forgive you your sins?

Stage Curtain

But it is written, eye has not seen, nor ear heard,
nor have entered into the heart of man the things
which God has prepared for those who love him.
____1 Corinthians 2:9 NKJV

A re you looking forward to the Lord's return as much as you do for the curtain to rise for an awaited play or for an important event to start?

Jesus said He was going away to prepare a place in His Father's house, that has many rooms, for everyone who love and live for Him. He also promised to come back and take them with Him (John 14:1–6).

People ask, "When is this going to happen?" No one knows. Only God knows the time He has set. It will be quick and without warning.

"Therefore keep watch, because you do not know on what day your Lord will come. But understand this: If the owner of the house had known at what time of night the thief was coming, he would have kept watch and would not have let his house be broken into. So you also must be ready, because the

Son of Man will come at an hour when you do not expect him" (Matthew 24:42-44)

Everyone who has accepted Christ as his Savior has the assurance, whether he is alive or not, that God will call him or her to meet Him in the air to be with Him forever.

"For the Lord himself will come down from heaven, with a loud command, with the voice of the archangel and with the trumpet call of God, and the dead in Christ will rise first. After that, we who are still alive and are left will be caught up together with them in the clouds to meet the Lord in the air. And so we will be with the Lord forever" (1 Thessalonians 4:16–17).

As a child of God are you watching for and eagerly anticipating the Lord's call to meet Him in the air to be with Him forever?

CPSIA information can be obtained
at www.ICGtesting.com
Printed in the USA
FFOW02n1128070416
23030FF